Raymond Feurstein

Home Spirit Home

Angels, and ministers of grace, defend us!
Be thou a spirit of health, or goblin damn'd.
Bring with thee airs from heaven, or blasts from hell.
Be thy intents wicked or charitable.
Thou com'st in such a questionable shape,
that I will speak to thee.
(Shakespeare's Hamlet, 1.4)

Written by:
Raymond A. Feurstein

Copyright © 2012 Raymond A. Feurstein
All rights reserved.
ISBN-13:978-1484058664
ISBN-10:1484058666

Graphic Artist: Terrie Brimingham
Editing By: Christine Wilson
Photographs by: Raymond Feurstein
Book cover photo by: Klaus Sandrini
www.sandrininet.info

DEDICATION

To those of you who have passed before me, and for those who support me in the living world. I dedicate this book to you.

JMEK

Contents

	Acknowledgments	4
	Foreword	5
1	The Beginning	7
2	The Spirit Inn	15
3	Brother Butch	20
4	Relations	27
5	A House with Spirit	39
6	The Shadow	48
7	The Song	53
8	Lizzy	57
9	The Journey	63
10	Fishing Buddies	71

ACKNOWLEDGMENTS

I would like to thank the following people for their contribution to this book. Mr. Peter Fuller and Family, The Old Women in the cellar, The Shadow Spirit, the Singing Woman, Elizabeth (Lizzy) and her dad Everett, My dad Joe, Uncle Ed and Leon, My brother Butch and all those spirits that have made this book possible.
May all of you find the peace you deserve.
If not, then
I hope you consider our humble house,

"Home Sweet Home"

FOREWARD

The following stories are life experiences in the paranormal. Specifically my spirit encounters. Since the age of five, spirit entities and ghostly apparitions have made it their job to make their presence known to me and other members of my family. These short stories are only a few of many instances where spirit activities have injected themselves into my life. The stories take place in various locations, but the common denominator is always me. The settings for these encounters include my childhood home, my family home, and the family owned cabin by the lake. The stories begin with a sting from a black wasp. That was the first time I died. For me, this event spurred many strange and curious encounters with the spirit world that have not stopped, even today.

There are many encounters to tell, but I selected these ten to start-off the series of short story books I plan to follow with. They all are instances and encounters individual unto themselves. So sit back, grab a talisman of your choice, and enjoy.

"The names of some of the people and places have been changed to protect their privacy."

Prologue

It all started with my near death experience at 5 years old. I am not sure "near death" accurately describes this experience. It should be death experience. You aren't "Near Death" you're dead! The trick is, being brought back to life. Therefore, I interpret my near death as a "Near Life" resurrection, and a lucky one at that. People who have "Near Life" resurrections, sometimes bring back stories of bright lights, angels and loved ones who have passed before them, taking their hands and guiding them back to their bodies to continue the life trek. None of which happened for me, as you will see in the upcoming story. It would seem, I brought back with me more than just a description of where I was and what I experienced, something else returned with me that day.

One: THE BEGINNING
The Day I Died

My name is Ray Feurstein. I am a 60 year old man, a recently retired communications engineer, a father of three and married to my best friend. We live in the upstate region of New York near the Albany Schenectady area. The series of stories you are about to read are a true account of spirit hauntings and paranormal activity. It may be hard for you to understand how one person could have so many paranormal experiences in their life. I'm not sure I fully understand it myself, but I will try to explain why there is a close connection with the paranormal, and the obsession the spirits seem to have with me.

Let's not get ahead of ourselves.
It started the day I died.
I was five years old.
It was summertime on the edge of fall. The days were cool and fast to night. Here is what happened on one of those endless fall nights when I was 5 years old. My older sister and I never did get along but after that day, it only got worse. My mother told me my sister always wanted a little sister and when I was born that just started an ongoing love hate relationship, oh well, sorry sis. My sister had an old dollhouse. Back then, most all toys were made of particle wood or a flimsy plastic. However, this dollhouse was constructed from solid wood. That afternoon my sister decided that she was too old to play with dollhouses. She took the house to the back yard and placed it by the garbage cans. Well that told me she didn't want it anymore, so it was time to play "Demolition Derby" with my father's hammer. Smash, bang, crash!! Man did I have fun. Pieces and parts of that house were all over the backyard. Later I found out that the dollhouse belonged to my favorite great aunt Lil. I wish I'd never destroyed the dollhouse because it had to be at least 100 years old.

Anyway, I left the carnage strewn all across the backyard. That afternoon my sister came home from school and went out back to retrieve the dollhouse from the garbage. I was inside with my mother baking cookies when we heard a scream come from the backyard. My mom and I went flying out to see what happened. I had forgotten about what I had done to the house. As we approached the door leading to the yard, my sister came bursting through the door screaming and yelling at me,

"You little brat! You stupid little brat!"

My mother stood spellbound at the sight of the utter destruction that lay before her in the battlefield we used to call our backyard. She told me to leave the mess to show my father when he came home. With that statement, it began to click that maybe it wasn't such a good idea to wreck the dollhouse. That evening, Dad came home from work and the second he stepped through the door, was met by my mom and sister squawking at him. They both laid into him about what I had done. He grabbed me and marched me out to the backyard. When he saw the amount of havoc I played on that innocent dollhouse he just stood and stared in disbelief.

How could a 5 year old boy do so much damage to such a well built toy? He asked me, "What were you thinking?" I said, "She threw it out and I played with it." Simple. What came next is very interesting. My dad told me that after supper I was to grab a garbage can and pick up every scrap of house I could find. So that's exactly what I did. It was "summer-fall" as we use to like to say. Not summer and not quite fall. The nights started to come sooner than normal so by 5:30pm it was dark out there. It took me about an hour to clean up all the mess. As I put the last piece of house in the can, my mom called me in to get ready for bed. I was to go to bed early that night. I started walking up the back steps to go into the house, and as I grabbed the doorknob, I felt a pinch and a burning behind my right ear. I was startled, to say the least and man did it hurt. I walked into the kitchen where my mother and sister where putting the dinner dishes away, the first one to me was my sister who, much to my surprise, looked very concerned. My mom was next. My dad had gone fishing and at that time, there were no cell phones. The look on both their faces was complete amazement and horror. I suppose I should describe what they saw.

In just a few words, I looked like the Michelin Tire Boy. If you've ever seen the ads before, this image should pretty much cover it. I started to feel nauseated and very sleepy. What had happened, if you haven't already guessed, a wasp stung me. Not an ordinary wasp but a black wasp, one of the most lethal species in North America It just so happens that I was allergic to wasp venom. No one knew until that night. To explain briefly what happens when a wasp or bee stings you. A person allergic to bee or wasp venom goes into what is referred to as Anaphylactic Shock. This causes your endocrine system to kick into high gear and release histamine to counteract the venom, which in turn causes your body to flood your system with liquid. You virtually drown in your own fluids. Nice Huh? The next thing I remember was my godfather at the front door, and a police car waiting outside ready to take me to the hospital. My sister and mother were crying. My godfather scooped me up and carried me to the police car. On the way to the hospital, the police officer asked me if I'd like the siren on. I nodded yes and on it came.

That was one of the last things I remember prior to waking up in the hospital. What I do remember during the time I was out is a bit fuzzy. I was sitting in a dark room with a single light above my head, kind of like a spot light shining down. The darkness wasn't something you could see, more over an inky blackness you could feel. All of a sudden, a gray black twister came out of the darkness and scooped me up. There was no noise, just a twister. I couldn't be sure, but it felt like there were people speaking to me inside the twister. What was being said to me wasn't real words more like thought words, mostly telling me what I can and can't do. Along with the voices inside the twister was the feeling that there were others outside, watching me, seemingly waiting for something to happen, an anxious feeling of dread. I only felt it when I tried to move outside the twister into the dark. It was almost as if the dark was alive. Have you ever had that feeling where someone or something was watching you, late at night while you were alone?

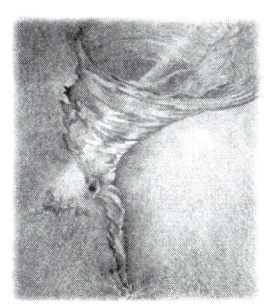

That's the feeling I had. I traveled for a while in the darkness, and occasionally I would see light spots, as if a single beam of light had been pointed at the ground. After a while, I saw myself heading towards one of those lit spots.

As I approached, I could see people milling around in the light; some were standing in the lighted area and others just between the light rim and the dark. As I moved closer, I could see children about my age playing with a whole bunch of puppies. I wasn't able to get down to play with the children because the twister kind of held me like a mother cradling a baby. However, I could lean out of the twister to touch the kids and puppies, in fact one little girl held a puppy up to me and said, "Hi, here you have one." At once, the twister began to move away from the light and the kids with the puppies. I reached out to grab a puppy but I was moving too fast. The light began to fade until there was only the dark nothingness. That is when I woke up. I was lying on my back looking up at a bright light when the image of a nurse and a doctor came into focus. They were saying something to me but I couldn't hear very well. My body was itchy and it ached all over. I can't remember how I got home that night or how long I was sick because of the incident. I overheard people saying how lucky I was and that I had died several times. Apparently, I died a couple of times on my way to the hospital and a couple of times while I was there. A short time after, is when things began to happen around our house. Strange things like voices, smells and bumps in the night. In the morning, we would find chairs moved around, cupboard doors open, and the contents thrown on the floor. The cats would walk around with the hair on their backs standing up. Sometimes they would run through the house as if someone was chasing them; their tails poofed out, wide eyed, and wired.

As time went by, people would come to visit but soon after they arrived, they would make excuses as to why they had to leave so abruptly. Foul odors would waft through the house causing my parents to scoot around opening doors and windows to chase out the stench. Even in the DEAD of winter. Many people including family members believe that something happened to open a corridor between the living world and the afterlife or where ever I went the night I died.

My mom and dad did say they couldn't remember any of these occurrences happening prior to my incident. The house I grew up in was my grandmother's before it became ours.

Our family lived in this house for over 100 years. I would have thought, in all that time there would have been at least one reported paranormal event.

Wouldn't you?

Prologue

Death holds no comfort for those who die with no knowledge of their own passing. Those lost souls set to wander through a pointless existence in a time remembered and out of place.

Two: The Spirit Inn

My childhood home was my Grandmother's and is not far from where I live today. When she passed away, it then became my mother's house. So you will see, my family has a history of living in houses previously owned by family. Here is a little tidbit about the history of my family's involvement in the paranormal.

I'd been told our family had quite a few "Sooth-Sayers" and "Fortune-Tellers." In olden days the meaning of these was quite different than today. They should have been referred to as Psychic Mediums. My Aunt Julie on my father's side told fortunes as a teenager all the way to her death at 68 years old. My Great Aunt Lillian on my mother's side was a sooth-sayer until her death at 86 years old as well.

Interesting fact, they both died at the same age and 18 years apart. One passed in July and the other in August. There has to be some numerology thing going on there but I'll leave that to someone else to get into. This story is about the house I grew up in as a child. Many strange events occurred during my life there. We would wake to find chairs set in the hallway with stuffed toys seated in them and sometimes candy. From time to time, late at night we heard a rocking chair that was in the attic rock back and forth for hours. The door to the attic came down from the ceiling with a staircase attached. I remember one time my dad Joe, went up in the attic to see if the window was open and possibly a draft was causing the chair to make the noise. But he found nothing. As soon as he opened the attic door, the chair stopped. No sooner did he come down from the attic and close the door, the chair would start back up. One time my dad laid the rocking chair on its side to see what would happen. For a short time the rocking stopped.

A few nights went by, we heard a bang, and then shortly after, the chair started rocking again. Eventually, we gave up and let whoever have their way. Out of exasperation, my dad finally just took the chair out of the attic. So you'd think that would be the end.

Oh no. Not this house.

The next sounds we heard were light, like a child's footsteps pacing back and forth. That was better than the chair. I tried bringing some of my toys up and leaving them there to see what would happen. It took a few days but they all found their way back down to my room piled together in a corner. I guess they weren't what this spirit wanted. I tried different toys to see if I could tell what age the spirit was. I left a doll there and that ended up hitting me in the head when I opened the attic door. The doll was placed inside the folded staircase ladder so when I dropped the door, the doll came tumbling out and bonked me on the head. Scared the living crap out of me too!

The only toy that was of any interest to the spirit was a can and a ball. We could hear the ball roll across the floor and into a can at the other end of the attic. The little spirit seemed to enjoy the game it played, but not all the time though. This may not be very scary but here's the killer. Sometimes when one of my family members took a shower, we would get out of the shower and find drawn in the steamed up mirror a Tic-Tack-Toe board. There would be an "O" drawn in the center square. We would place an "X" in one of the other boxes. Then leave and wait a while to see what happens. No other marks would appear. Only one other time did I find a second "O" placed in another box.
I kept playing but I never saw any other marks appear. This happened a few times before it stopped all together. Once one encounter or occurrence started and stopped, another would follow. It was as if the house was a revolving door for spirit activity. They would come in, interact, and leave. The only spirit that stayed was our little attic guest.

To this day, the ball still rolls from one end of the attic to the other. My mother passed away a year or more now. We are in the process of selling her house.

I hope whoever buys it will enjoy...

"The Spirit Inn."
They check in after they've checked out!

Prologue

There is no describing a voice from the other side.
Except, when you hear one you never forget the sound.
Ever..........

Three: Brother Butch

This story is a little darker than the rest. I've included some background that leads up to the rest of the story; I felt that leaving anything out such as the history and what led up to the incident would make this story a bit confusing. When I was younger, I lived about two blocks away from where I am now. As you know, the house I grew up in was my Grandmother's home. I never knew my grandmother; she died the year I was born. The story begins when I was 12 years old and returning home after attending a church sponsored outing to a baseball game in New York City. I was an altar boy in our church and the priests organized the trip for all the altar boys and their fathers. As we made the turn on the street leading to the school, I could see a whole bunch of people standing around waiting to pick up their kids.

I noticed that there were two priests standing there waiting as well. As we exited the bus, one of the priests immediately came and asked my father to go with him for a moment. The other priest grabbed me and kept me from hearing what was being said. I was a little afraid because at that time, you could say, I was a bit of a rebel. I thought I was in trouble for something I had done. I couldn't remember anything recently I did though. I guess because of past mischief, I figured there must be something and I will find out soon enough. My dad finally came over to me and took my hand. We said our goodbyes then headed for home. As we walked, he didn't say much at all. Just as we rounded the corner to our house, Dad turned to me and said, "Just remember Ray, we had a good time today. This was a good day for you and me. No matter what happens today, don't forget that please." I thought, "What a curious statement," especially for my father. We lived about a block from the church and school, so it was a short walk home. I must have taken that route dozens of times.

It didn't seem half as long as it did that night. When we finally made it to the front door of our home, and was able to look through the window, I could see a whole bunch of people inside. "Man!" I thought, "I must have done something bad!" We went inside. From across the room I could see my mother was crying, as were some of the other people. My godfather appeared out of nowhere and took me out to the backyard. He sat me down and told me my older brother Butch had died that day. My brother had been murdered in Troy New York, a city just outside of Albany where he lived. My older brother was living there for his work. They said he drowned that afternoon while we were away. The interesting part of this for me was that Butch drowned. He was an expert swimmer and even taught me how to swim. My parents knew that fact, which was partially why it had been deemed a murder and not an accident. The next few weeks included a wake, and the funeral, all the while people were coming in and out of our house in a seemingly unending procession.

My mother was out of it, crying all the time while calling out my brother's name. One day my dad came to my sister, my other brother, and me asking if we had smelled anything out of the ordinary. Mostly by the staircase leading to the upstairs. We had all noticed there was an odor. A cologne smell. *Blue Blaze*. The type of aftershave my older brother Butch used to wear. It only appeared in the staircase and was very heavy. The odor increased in intensity to where we almost couldn't bare the smell. One day I was returning home from school, walking with a bunch of friends; doing what kids do after school. I was about a block away when I saw one of the priests from my church coming out of my house. I hurried home to see what was going on. I was told by my parents, we would be leaving our house to stay with my godfather and mother for a few days. The priest would be performing an exorcism that night. It appeared that my older brother was still here.

From how it was explained to me, my mother's unwillingness to let my brother go caused him to stay. The exorcism was completed and the odor went away. A week went by and still no odor. One night while everyone was fast asleep, I awoke to the ringing of the phone outside my bedroom door. The sound the phone made was strange. The only way to describe it was lazy-like. Since the phone was on the desk at the top of the stairs nearest my room, I picked up the phone and said, "Hello?"
The voice on the other end said,

"Hi Ray! This is Butch. Tell Mom and Dad I'm alright and you be good." I said "OK."

Then we both said goodbye. I was still half-asleep so I went back to bed. Some of you may remember not so long ago, if someone called you from a long ways away, the connection sounded full of static and the voice seemed a bit distant. That is how the voice on the other end sounded to me.

I woke up the next morning, remembered the incident, and thought I dreamt the whole thing. I dressed for school then went downstairs to the kitchen. My mom was cooking breakfast and my dad was reading the newspaper. I sat down and started to eat when my father asked me,
"Who was on the phone last night?"
I almost choked on my eggs, but I said,
"No one."
I knew how much sadness my brother's death brought to the family. I was afraid if I said anything about what had happened they would be mad at me. It wasn't until 40 years later; I was sitting in the kitchen having a cup of coffee with my mother, when I shared that phone conversation. I was married and Dad had passed away. I would have breakfast with my mother a few times a week. One morning in particular I decided to ask her if she remembered back when Butch died. During the time she and Dad had the house exorcised. Specifically, the time when the phone rang late one night.

She said she remembered that night.

So I told her what actually happened, and why I didn't say anything that morning to Dad and her.

She said she understood and believed me. Maybe I should have told my parents then. Nevertheless, it felt like the right time when I finally did.

Prologue

There's a calm over there that keeps you wrapped in a cocoon of joy and peace, a feeling in life you have never felt. You want to stay but must go and complete what you've started out to do in life. Whatever that may be...

Four: Relations

It was 1969, I was 17 years old and a junior in high school, the captain of the track team, and had a weekend Rock and Roll band that played all the schools in town. I was dating a real nice girl and was preparing for our junior prom.
I was on top of the world. A few days before the prom, I was not feeling very well and had to stay home from school to recoup. Of course, I was pissed off because I thought I might miss the dance, but my father told me it was just the flu and would be right as rain for Saturday. It was Monday, the week of the prom, and man was I in the dumps. I had a high fever, sweats, nausea, and a pain that shot from my groin to the middle of my back. It felt as though someone had stuck a red-hot poker in my gut. My father gave me some Milk of Magnesia to help with the nausea.

I no sooner drank the potion when all hell broke loose. The pain was so intense I couldn't breathe. My dad grabbed me and brought me to the family GP for a look-see. We were standing on the stoop of the office waiting for the doctor to arrive when all at once I blacked out. When I opened my eyes, there stood Dr. Casella. He was saying something but I couldn't focus through the pain. The next thing I knew I was in the back seat of our car racing to the emergency room. There were three people waiting for us when we arrived at the hospital, they put me on a gurney and wheeled me into the examination room. The Intern told the nurses to call the surgeon and get the operating room ready for his arrival. He told my dad that it would be about an hour before the surgeon would arrive and the preliminary diagnosis was Appendicitis. The nurse gave me a sedative then wheeled me down to the pre-op area to wait for the surgeon. I was only there a few minutes when all of a sudden all the pain and nausea disappeared. I felt great! I told my dad that I was feeling better and the pain was gone.

He called for the nurse, told her what I had said then they both rushed out of the room. The next instant, the intern charged back in the room with an orderly to strap me down to the gurney. We raced down the hall and crashed through the operating room doors, where we were met by a posse of masked hombres ready to do battle. One nurse placed a mask on my mouth and nose and soon I was in slumber land. I can't tell how long I was out but there were instances I could feel myself hovering over the operating room, looking down at my body lying on the gurney with people huddled around me intently doing something, I'm not sure what though. In and out, up and down, this seemed to go on forever, until I found myself in a lighted room full of sound and people. The sound was nothing I had ever heard before and for the life of me, I couldn't begin to describe. The only word that may come close is, "Joy" or "Joyful."

It was as if I was inside happiness and contentment. The people were all standing around talking to each other and the sound seemed to be the chatter from them. So beautiful, so soothing, like something from a dream. They looked right at me, smiled, and then went on chatting as though I belonged there. I would like to describe how things looked to me while I was there. If you have ever put a clear drinking glass to your eye and looked through it, this is the vision I experienced. My peripheral vision was distorted and a little fuzzy, but straight on was clear as a bell. I walked around and looked for a door, a wall, or a window, something of substance to touch. There were some vague images of chairs, tables, and pieces of buildings, mostly light and people. One of them started walking towards me and I froze in my tracks. Not knowing what the person was going to say or do made me a little anxious. A voice came from the person that seemed to be all around me and blanketed me in calm.

The person appeared to be a woman in her 40's, long light brown hair and beautiful sparkling blue eyes. She took my hand and led me to a group that was standing nearby. They all greeted me and asked how I felt. I told them "Pretty damn good." They laughed and for a time I felt at home and the most relaxed I could remember. We were standing there for a while, when the woman took my hand once more and said, "You need to go back now," it is time." I was a little confused and something inside me didn't want to go. I said to the woman, "Do I have to?" I want to stay with you." The woman just smiled and led me to a clearing. She gave me a hug and said, "You are a good person Ray; remember that as you travel through your life", "Please tell your mother I said it's alright now, Tommy is here with me doing just fine." With that, I felt a tug and at once I was back in the operating room again looking up at the nurses and doctors with their eyes wide open as in shock. I said, "Hey," What's Up Doc?"

I thought it was funny. They all just smiled and said, "How do you feel?"

I said "Pretty dam good."

Then I smiled, knowing that wasn't the first time I had said that line. The feeling I had on the other side stayed with me for a few days.

I couldn't tell anyone about the experience because I didn't know how to without sounding a bit crazy. I was in the hospital for about two weeks. The scar that was a part of me now stretched from one side of my abdomen to the other. My parents told me my appendix had ruptured and I had been poisoned by the toxic waste from the abscessed organ. When it burst and the pain went away, that was the sign that I was in critical danger due to this poisoning. They had to open me up to clean out all the poison and remove the appendix. This took a few hours to do. During that time I had died twice. My system and body went into septic shock. They had to resuscitate and use a heart defibrillator on me to try to bring me back. I was gone for three minutes. It seemed a whole lot longer to me, but it was hard to mark time there.

I really didn't care to because it was so nice and peaceful. I guess that's where they get "Rest In Peace."

It was a week later and I was home still convalescing when my mother sat down next to me on the couch. She just sat there and stared at me for a while. It was kinda spooky. She finally spoke up in a shaky sort of voice and asked me what happened while I was under anesthesia? She really wanted to say," While I was dead." I told her my story, how I was in a lighted place with a crowd of people and beautiful sounds. She again stared at me and said, "who did you meet there?" I told her there were a lot of people but one woman actually made contact with me. I described her to my mom, as soon as the words came out of my mouth my mother started to tear up. I stopped talking knowing that what I was saying was upsetting her for some unknown reason. I asked her what the matter was. She replied, "While you were out, you said "good-bye grandma."

I told her I didn't recognize the woman at all and didn't recall saying anything of the sort to her as I left. My mom then told me she heard me say "Rose." That was her mother's name. I vaguely recall the woman telling me that, by now it was all getting a little fuzzy and hard to remember. My mother got up from the couch and ran upstairs. A few moments later she came down with a box of pictures. She sat there next to me and pawed through them until she found the one she was searching for. She took it out of the box, cupped it in her hands looking at it for a short time, and then handed the picture to me. "Is this the woman that you met?" She said with a shaking voice. I looked at the picture and sure enough that was the woman with the golden brown hair and sparkling eyes, just as I saw her that day. My mom never showed me the pictures because they were a hurt she couldn't bear. You see just before her mother passed away, her and her mom had a horrific fight. She never did say what the fight was about, just that things were said, and that same night her mother passed in her sleep.

She never had the chance to tell her she was sorry for the hurtful things she said. Or to tell her mom she loves her. We sat for a while just looking at people in the photos when I came across one single picture. An old black and white, very faded and cracked, of a young man in his twenties standing by a 1937 black Studebaker sedan. It was winter right in front of our house. I gave the photo to my mother and asked who it was. She said, "No one you would ever know." For whatever reason I blurted out, "Tommy?"

I thought she would fall off the couch in a faint. Her eyes drew wide, her face lost all color, and her mouth hung open like she was catching flies. She looked at me as if I had two heads and asked, "Where did you hear that name?" I said I remembered something her mom said to me while I was with her. I recalled the conversation to my mother saying, "You are a good person Ray; remember that as you travel through your life, and tell your mother I said it's alright now, Tommy is here with me doing just fine."

I don't know why, at that moment I remembered what was said to me that day. It just popped into my mind as though someone gently whispered the thought in my ear. My mother sat on the edge of the couch, broke out into tears, and for a long time said nothing. I waited until she was ready to speak and when she did, I couldn't believe what came out. My mother told me Tommy was her older brother that went missing when she was 20 years old. He was hiking with a friend up in the Adirondacks for the weekend. The friend made it back but Tommy didn't. As the story goes, they were camped for the night, Eddie; Tommy's friend went to fetch more wood for the campfire, when Eddie returned Tommy was gone. Eddie search all night and into the next morning before coming home to report Tommy missing. There was a two-day search party organized but nothing came up, there were no signs of Tommy ever being at the campsite. Of course, this was the 1930's; there were little resources available to perform the type of search and rescues we have today.

Tommy became one more person lost in the Adirondacks. I guess my mother was close to her brother, and took it very hard when he never came back. I did find out what the argument was about that fateful night her mom passed away. My Great Aunt Lil, the fortune-teller, called a week before to tell my grandmother not to allow Tommy to go on the camping trip, something bad was going to happen. My grandmother ignored the warning and let him go all the same. My mother, knowing how accurate my aunt always was with this sort of thing, begged my grandmother, her mom, to listen to my aunt Lil. So you can imagine now the conversation that ensued after Tommy's disappearance. I could never understand how it would feel to lose someone like that with no closure as to whether they were alive or dead.

All those years with no closure, no way of knowing what happened to him. Now at least there is finality to his disappearance. He is with his mom on the other side doing well as it were. I've been asked, if I am afraid of death or dying. I say no, not at all.

The little knowledge I have of the afterlife gives me comfort in knowing someone who loves me will be there waiting to take my hand once more, and lead me to peace for all eternity. Not knowing how long that could be.

I think I'll pack a lunch.

Prologue

I can't explain the feeling of interacting with a spirit, let alone multiple spirit entities. Having them talking and touching you without being able to do a thing about it. And they know it.

Five: A House with Spirit

This next story takes place in the house I am currently living. I have lived in this house for 34 years with my wife and three children. The property dates back to the mid 1800's. A man named Peter Fuller built this house in 1904; he also built, owned, and operated a gristmill, which was not far from our home. Peter Fuller was the main supplier of flour in the area. The mill was built on the hill leading from the downtown area to the city. His house was at the top of the hill less than a quarter mile away. He owned the property for about 50 years and with his wife Margaret Fuller, had one son, Alfred, and two daughters, Mary and Katie. Peter was born on January 23rd, 1834 and died March 12th, 1912. William Fuller was his brother and business partner in the gristmill.

William kept the house for 45 years before selling it to Donald Munster, Peter Fuller's first cousin. Donald Munster then sold the house to us. After moving into our new home on May 16, 1975, we found out that Donald Munster was our cousin as well. So you see, the house and property had been family owned since it was built. One day I decided to go to the attic to see what, if anything, had been left behind after Don Munster had moved. I found an old cast iron gas fireplace heater, some books, and a box of tin type photographs. i had shown the photos to my parents to see if they knew any of the people in the pictures. Among many of them were my Great Grandparents' portraits. That was so cool. We now have them hanging in the stairwell leading upstairs. Now you know a little background to the rest of this story. From the day I moved in, up to the present day, there have been many strange and unexplained happenings. My older son Mike was the first to come to my wife and me about the visitations. I asked him not to share this information with his younger siblings;

it might scare them. Little did anyone know, everyone in the family had seen these apparitions at least once but never told a Soul. Since I was very small, I had always believed in ghosts and spirits. For many years, my children, mostly my daughter, often came to tell us about the people that would come into their rooms at night and speak to them. We assumed it was dreams or half sleep remembrance. As time went by, the frequency of events and the weird happenings became more prevalent. Dressers and beds would shake, the chains hanging from the mirrors would rattle, and the windows would bang and tap. I know windows banging may not be signs of spirit activity. Normally I would have to agree with you, but the banging or tapping sound was rhythmic in nature. The tapping sound could never be mistaken for wind or trucks driving by the house. The sound took on a rhythmic cadence of five equally spaced taps declining in volume as they played out. Most often the tapping would be on the window right by our bed. Many times the tapping continued until I would say,

"Please stop, you're keeping me awake."
All at once the tapping would stop.
Weird Huh?
Well that's not all. As my daughter grew older and started entering puberty (between 12 and 15 years) the spirit activity increased. I read somewhere that spirits often gravitate towards young adolescent women. There is some sort of energy young adolescent women give off. Anyway, more distinctive and recurring goings-on started to ramp up. Now we were hearing bumps in the night. The back door would open and close, mostly around two in the morning on Saturday and Sunday nights. You could hear distinctive footsteps coming up the stairs and ending at my daughter's bedroom door. At times, my daughter would wake up and hear someone talking to her. She would hear them whispering, "Shut the window" or "Turn off the fan," and sometimes just her name. The tapping on the window and the shaking of the dressers became more violent as time went on.

The interesting part was, every time I said out loud, "Please stop," Whatever they were doing they stopped! Most of the time anyway. My daughter Kira described the one spirit as a tall thin man with a long coat, long straight hair wearing a brimmed hat. Something else, it looked as though he had a bottle of beer in his hand. The dark man stood in the corner of her room just inside the shadow and just beyond the light looking out her bedroom window. Occasionally he would turn and smile at her. She seldom felt threatened or afraid. One Saturday afternoon my daughter decided to go to the library and look up Peter Fuller and his mill. We hoped she would find a picture of him. She got lucky and there he was, long hair, hat and coat. Just as my daughter had described him. The article stated that Peter Fuller was a prominent businessman. Had two younger daughters named Katie and Mary and a son named Alfred. Not much about his wife Margaret though. The mother of his children, Peter's lifelong mate, had very little mentioned about her.

You would think there would be more. Margaret is only just mentioned on the family gravestone. I thought that curious. I went back many times to hunt for more information on Mr. Fuller and his family and each time there were only references to his son and daughters, still nothing about his wife. Peter lost his family in the late 1800's because of an influenza epidemic, which happened to families back then. Peter Fuller and his family are buried in a nearby church cemetery. My daughter wants to visit the gravesite some time. For some odd reason, I am not ready to do that yet. Peter is not the only ghosty in our house. There are at least four more. A man that just walks around stomping his feet, a small animal type spirit, a shadow being and an old woman that lives in the basement. I had built a kids room down in one of the areas in the cellar. That way my children could have friends over, make as much noise as they wanted, and have sleepovers there.

Quite often, one or more of the friends that slept over, saw the old woman. She seemed to like the kids and just enjoyed watching over them. You'll know when she's around because of the scent of vanilla. As soon as you smell the vanilla, she appears. She has a housedress on, you know the type, one piece from the neck to the floor. It has long sleeves with little pink and yellow flowers on a beige background with doily type ruffles on the neck and sleeves. The little animal spirit is not so nice. We were never able to get a good look at that one. It would appear all the rattling and thumping was coming from that spirit. My youngest son Eric had that spirit in his room more often than not. It was small and made low growling sounds. Eric told us the spirit stood by the door that led to the attic. He also said this spirit, whatever it was, had red glowing eyes. Eric described the entity to be more like a little animal than a human spirit. Through the years my children lived with us, there were many spirit manifestations. As soon as the kids left, one by one, to go out into the world, the incidents began to fade.

I installed vinyl windows, which replaced the old double hung windows, and the tapping soon stopped as well. A while later my wife bought a wooden sign and hung it in the upstairs bathroom. One morning I was in taking a shower. All at once, the tapping started again but this time on the wooden sign.

All I said then was,

"Welcome Back."

There were many spirit happenings during that time, so it's hard to write about all of them. I typically read books that are not trying to convince me that spirits exist as much as books that tell the "why for's" of how some spirits act. As I have come to understand, there are particular and distinctive traits to different types of spirits and their actions.

I had mentioned there were only four spirits in the house. I neglected to tell you about the shadow that runs around here still. From what I have read, corner of the eye type appearances are normal.

This shadow looms only by the stairs and lingers for long periods of time. We see the shadow spirit often. I have kept a log of the spirit events. They seem to coincide with stress in one or more of my family's lives.

The more the stress the more frequent the appearances.
Go figure.

Prologue

A bump in the night, a wisp of cold air across your face, and a feeling of uncontrollable dread sears your soul to the bone. A quick glimpse of someone moving and a shadow appears out of the corner of your eye. In the same instant, it's gone!

Six: The Shadow

I left off the last story talking about the shadow being that skulks around here and there. No real mischief though, just popping up late at night. Whatever or whoever it is, didn't need any contact with us. So we thought. I wish to share with you a little more about my early family history. As long as I can remember, my parental family was deeply involved with spiritualism and mysticism. Two of my aunts were practicing Sooth-Sayers or Fortune-Tellers as it were, not to be confused with the Psychic Mediums of today. My Great Aunt Lillian foretold my older brother Butch's (Joe Jr.) death about three months before it happened. So you see, my family, past and present, are no strangers to spirit encounters.

I would first like to tell you a story about the house we presently live in. The dining room sits directly under my wife and mine's bedroom. The living room is underneath my daughter's bedroom. One night while I was working on a project with my younger son Eric on the computer, that was set up next to the fireplace in the dining room, there was a banging noise in the upper right corner of the ceiling. It was just about where the door to my daughter's room would be. There were three raps on the ceiling. Then something that sounded like a squirrel scurrying across the space between the ceiling and upstairs floor. The sound ran right across the edge of the ceiling out towards the back door. After the incident, a horrible stink filled the room. I shot a look at my son and he said, "It wasn't me!" Eric and I sat there in shock at first and then we just shrugged our shoulders and started to go back to what we were doing. A moment later, I turned around and there stood my daughter Kira, as white as a sheet, sweating and shaking all over. She was mouthing something but no sound came out.

The look on her face was sheer terror! I sat her down and asked what the matter was. Kira said that she had been sitting in her room doing homework and heard a loud banging on the door. She said she thought it was one of us so she opened the door to yell at us but no one was there. In the instant that she opened the door, it was jerked out of her hand and slammed shut. A voice made a low guttural growl at her and everything on her dresser began to shake violently. She ran out of the room and downstairs to me. I believe this entity is the shadow spirit we see at times. Each time the entity appears, something is shaken, or a noise is heard. This spirit, up until then, had never done anything but skulk around near the front door. This event wasn't the end for that night however. Later that night, around 2:00am the back door opened and shut harder than ever. We heard a loud bang and the sound of slow and deliberately hard footsteps coming up the stairs to the bedrooms.

Someone wasn't happy and wanted everyone to know it. For about a week or so, personal items were disappearing from one part of the house and reappearing in a different room all together; in some instances became permanently missing. The TV would turn on and change channels by itself. We had to unplug many of the electrical appliances to stop from being woken up every night. At the time, there was nothing majorly stressing or out of the ordinary going on in the family. It always appeared when any of our family members were experiencing stress, the spirit sightings and events would become more aggressive. This episode didn't fit the normal spirit profile for my family or the house. In addition, we had been locked out of our house on numerous occasions and had to be sure to take keys with us every time we went outside. Even If we just went for the mail, we needed the keys. Whoever or whatever it was did not want us to come back in. I am not sure why, but after a time all the crazy things tapered off and life went back to normal.

Well, as normal as it could be living with spirits in the house.

Or as we like to refer to them as:

"The Living-Impaired."

Prologue

Spirits talking, screaming, and groaning are para "Normal" occurrences. However, a spirit singing is not normal and is quite unsettling. It is a tune not soon forgotten.

Seven: The Song

The strangest encounter so far was the night the spirits decided to become vocal. It was November or December time frame, Holiday season. The most active accounts of spirit happenings occurred between September to December. Don't misunderstand me; there were plenty of spirit encounters during the year, it just seemed to peak around this time. I read somewhere that many people experience depression and anxiety during this time as well as a rise in suicides and violence had been reported. "Tis the season to be jolly" may not apply for all. I have a cousin who works in the psychiatric wing in a large hospital nearby. She has told me they have to increase the medication and security for many of the patients due to this seasonal outbreak of depression. Strange as it may seem, most of the patients don't really know what time of year it is let alone that it's the Holiday Season, but they react all the same. Anyway, on with the tale... It was around 2:00am on a Friday night or Saturday morning as it were. Our bedroom is positioned directly above the dining room and because my wife was not feeling well, she decided to go down to sleep on the couch so she didn't disturb me. I was awoken by a sound. Half asleep, I got out of bed and headed down stairs. The sound was a voice singing a song of sorts. Six notes. The voice must have sung the little tune more than once because as I was waking up I caught the end of the tune and then again while I was almost downstairs in the living room. It was so loud and clear. It felt like the voice was coming from everywhere, especially the dining room. I looked in the dining room but it was empty except our two cats. One was sitting on the floor and the other on the dining room table. Both cats were looking straight up at the light in the middle of the ceiling.

The light is directly underneath the middle of our bed. By then my wife was half-awake. I asked her if she heard anything. She said, "Someone was singing."

Being a musician myself, I was able to remembered the tune the next day; the note's were very distinctive and were arranged like so,

"B – Bflat – E, A – Aflat – D".

The spirit sang this combination of notes more than once. That little tune has haunted me ever since. Her voice sounded melancholy but strong and clear. This incident never happened again but I will tell you this, I'll never forget that sound. All I can say about the experience is the sound was otherworldly in nature. The next day I talked with my wife about the encounter. We spent that whole day trying to find a logical explanation for the voice. Never did find one. Probably never will. I spoke with our neighbors and asked if they were up late the night before with a radio or TV on; none of them had been up late. The cats were the real stickler.

They sat for quite a while staring up at the light in the dining room. For weeks after, both cats would come into the dining room, stop and look up at the light for a few moments then go on about their business. Frequently animals and young children see things as adults we won't see. Yeah I didn't say we can't see, I said we won't see. Kids and animals have a knack for seeing these apparitions we adults refuse to see. Must be the loss of innocence or something like that. All I can say is, since that night, a different feeling has come over this house. Believe it or not, it is a peaceful and much warmer atmosphere now. I realize how crazy all of this must sound. But unless you live here or have had experiences of your own, there is no way to describe the feeling of a spirit encounter such as this. We are planning to have a séance some time soon. This should prove very interesting indeed.

So remember keep your spirits high and your encounters to a minimum.

Prologue

She stands on the edge of the woods just before the beach, looking. Maybe to a future she'll never have or know. Or a lifetime long forgotten. Who knows. All that's left is to live out those last few moments she can remember, in hopes that time will catch up someday...... and give her peace.

Eight: Lizzy

In one way or another, the paranormal has always been a part of my family. As I've said before, many of my relatives were psychic. My father was a practicing Druid. I found this fact out many years later, after his death. The Druids of his day were not the dark ones of Celtic lore, but more a group of men that practiced the earth rites and celebrations, kind of like the Wicca religion. Only one of our family members dabbled in the dark arts (Seven-Book Moses) my Great Uncle James. But that's a tale for another time. This story happened at a lake in the Adirondack Mountains. My family has owned property at the lake since 1946. I spent much of my life up at the lake; it is an incredibly beautiful area.

However, it wasn't always a lake. It was a valley with many small homesteads, hamlets, and villages. Before flooding the valley to create the lake, they moved the villages and the homesteads along with all the graves to another location. So everyone thought. During the summer season, my friend Ron and I used to go down to the water to ski and swim, all the normal things you would do at a lake. Often we would go to the shore around 6 or 7pm to watch the sun set over the mountains. The afterglow or twilight of the setting sun would cast eerie shadows in the woods. The dark contrast of the woods against the dimly lit shore caused the entrance to the beach to look like a portal to another world. Often, we would see a figure standing at the edge of the woods just before the light of the beach. It was a young girl about 16 years old wearing a sundress. The dress was beige with small blue flowers on it.

"Forget-Me-Not's" I believe.

She had long blonde hair with a slight figure, not skinny just petite and very pretty.

Each time we saw her, she would turn around, look over her shoulder at us, and smile. Each time we would hurry our pace to catch up to her. She would become more and more transparent as we approached. As we reached the spot where the girl in the sundress was standing she would completely disappear. What was interesting about this encounter was that each time we saw her; she looked at us and smiled. When she disappeared she left the air filled with the scent of Lilacs. The aroma lingered for several moments and then it too would disappear. We saw her many times throughout our life there. We began to call her Lizzy. She seemed to like that. As we became older the appearances grew less frequent. Other interests began to take up more of our time such as, girlfriends who occupied our thoughts, and our wallets. We began to see less and less of her until one day, in the summer of 1971, the year I was drafted into military service that she reappeared again. The Vietnam War was still raging at that time.

My parents decided to put a going away party together for me up at the cabin with a bunch of my friends. My vacation home buddy Ron came from Buffalo to say goodbye as well. That evening we took a walk down to the beach as we had done so many times before, and there she was. However this time she was facing us and seemed sad. We approached, talking to her, telling her we missed her all these years and it was good to see her again. Interesting enough, she was facing us but as we approached she didn't disappear.

Lizzy stood there looking at us with this sad and worried look on her face. Somehow, she seemed to know that I was going away to a war. We stopped short of her so as not to scare or chase her away, although it didn't appear that she wanted to go anywhere. All three of us stood there not speaking until Ron said to her, "Lizzy, why do you look so sad?" We stood a little while longer and she put her hands together over her heart, smiled once more at us then turned to face the lake and vanished.

The Lilac scent continued to linger for along time after. Ron wondered if it were possible Lizzy missed us too. Ron felt that maybe she may have missed me the most. I was 20 at the time. By the way, Ron and I researched the settlement that was just off the shore from our beach. Scottstown was the name of the little hamlet. There was an article describing a fever epidemic that took many of the children and older folks' lives around the late 1800's. About 50 people died of this fever. One was a young girl about the age of 16 or 17 named Elizabeth. We hadn't known this until after we named our friend Lizzy and I'm not sure how we came up with her name. Maybe it was on a whisper of the wind in our ears, or on the breath of a cool summer night's frost. It just felt right I suppose, or maybe she told us in her own way. She appeared to me once more, the day I returned from the service.
September 23, 1973.
It was a beautiful Indian summer day. The leaves had turned and the lake was like a pooled mirror.

She came to me at dusk, on the edge of the woods, just after the sun had slipped behind the mountains and the beach was lit by the afterglow of the setting sun.

Her dress, her smile, and the scent of Lilacs.

At that moment, I wished I could put my arm around her, but then all at once she vanished. I have never seen her again. Every once in awhile I'll catch the scent of lilacs and know she is still there.

Prologue

Time stands still and a journey that should have taken hour's turns into an endless loop of a single moment in time. Playing over and over again, your world without end.

Nine: The Journey

My father built our cabin that is located in the beautiful Adirondack mountain range, with help from my godfather Jim, Uncle Ed and a friend next door to us named Leon. The property includes a private beach right across from an island smack dab in the middle of the lake area. It is absolutely beautiful there. The previous story described a young girl about 16 – 17 years old who use to visit my friend Ron and me at the lake. This story is a supplement to that encounter. This lake was once a valley that housed many towns, villages, and hamlets. Before they flooded the valley, all the towns and villages were relocated along the projected outer shoreline. The project began around 1930. It took 5 to 6 years to complete the dam and relocation. The residents along with the cemeteries had to be moved to higher ground.

Our beach just happens to be right in front of one of these hamlets. A few hundred yards to the northeast of the settlement was the cemetery. The houses were not taken down and the foundations still stand just under the surface of the water. We would scuba dive down to them occasionally and find coins, old clay smoking pipes and assorted household bottles and farm tools. These little villages had been there since the early 1800's and some before that. The age of the graves dated back to many of the early settlers. Indian artifacts had been found in and around the lake for years as well. These facts always lend to a rich spirit active area. So on with the encounters. We have a fire pit down on the beach. Ron and I used to build a fire late at night, sit on the beach, roast marshmallows, talk about girls and just relax. The canopy of stars made you feel like you were on top of the world. There are no city lights to drown out the starlight so you could see the Milky Way very clearly. It is truly amazing.

One night, around midnight while Ron and I were sitting by the fire, there was a noise behind us in the woods. At this time of night, the only sounds you would hear were the constant lapping of small waves from the dark water and the occasional slap of a fish jumping to eat a bug. Not much more. But there was something different about this sound. We knew everyone who lived around us, but there was no one out that night. The sound we heard was a shuffling of feet. It wasn't unusual to have a bear or raccoon running around. But this was different. The shuffling was rhythmic, like someone slowly walking, and dragging their heavy, plodding feet. As if they had been carrying a heavy load a long ways. We sat very quiet and listened. The sound became louder and louder and it appeared to be more than one person walking. We watched and waited to see who it could be coming out of the woods. The footsteps changed to a soft thud, thud, thud as they hit the beach. They passed right by us about 20 feet or so. The firelight was dim but we didn't dare move to add more wood to make it brighter. We sat frozen in our seats. Both Ron and I knew that it wasn't a neighbor.

Accompanying the footsteps was a labored and stressed breathing sound. Like whoever they were had been walking a long time getting here. Later, Ron and I dug up old maps and layouts of the original placement of the villages. We found that our property just happened to be a trail from the road to a small settlement called Scottstown. This little hamlet was located on the northeastern tip of the island that lies directly in front of us. We uncovered this information while researching the name of the girl we saw on the beach which we happened to name Lizzy. We figured the footsteps must be the people from the tiny settlement trying to make it back to their homes. It wasn't the first time this sound had been heard. One night, after having a fire on the beach, my brother and his girlfriend came up from the lake complaining to my parents about Ron and me tramping around the woods. My mother told him that we were in bed all the while. Quite often, Ron and I would sit on the beach late at night; we could see lights that appeared to glow under the water out near the cemetery area.

We never understood what could cause such a phenomena. We had thought it was starlight reflecting down on the water. The night skies were so clear and bright the stars looked like pinholes punched in a black cloth. But star reflection is just that. The lights moved in a line from the shoreline to the area where the cemetery was reported to be, and then they vanished. The lights were bluish white and left a streak behind them as they moved through the water. The next day I moseyed down to the beach as usual to make sure the fire was out. Ron was already there. He called to me before I stepped on the beach, told me to cross over to his property, and climb over the rocks to him. I did just that. As I reached him, I found Ron looking down at the sand pointing out the marks he had found. It looked as though a troop of people moved through that same spot we heard the sounds the night before. Sure, you're going to say my father, mother or my other siblings made the marks in the sand.

But no! We were the first ones to the beach that morning. Remember our property and the beach is private. Then no one would trespass on another person's land without asking first. A little different today. The marks in the sand led down to the water's edge then disappeared. We noticed that only one pair of prints came back out of the water and headed towards the road. We asked around town and found a couple of older people, a sister and brother, Anna and Seth Ulman. They were about 80 plus years old at the time. The brother and sister told us their parents lived during the flooding of the valley. Seth continued saying, "We were one of the first residents relocated." They told us that their father was a courier for the towns and villages that surrounded the lake. Their dad would shuttle town's people back and forth from Jonesville to the trail that led out to a hamlet near what is now the island area. The small settlement was called Scottstown, although we knew the name from our earlier research. Seth remembered going with his dad to bring shop goods to the village.

His dads name was Everett Ulman. I don't know if the returning footprints were Everett Ulman or not. I do know that I will never forget that sound and the breathing, or the lights in the water. I neglected to mention, not all the dead may have made it out of that valley before it was flooded. Contractors were hired to exhume the bodies and replace the headstones at the Weller Township Cemetery. In their haste to move the towns and cemeteries, some of the bodies never made it to their final resting place. So the story goes. Allegedly, this fact was uncovered by an historian about 43 years ago while he was researching into the exodus prior to the flooding. Notes uncovered documentation written by the contracting company's personnel outlining how many villages and hamlets had been moved. The notes also allude to the fact there may not have been enough time to exhume all the graves so only the tombstones were taken. There were many little settlements that had their own small cemeteries.

If you've ever taken a ride in the county, you would see these small family plots by the side of the road. One of these sites supposedly not completely moved was the Scottstown settlement. The same cemetery Seth's father had been buried. We never told the siblings about the encounter. We did ask if they knew of a young girl about 16 or 17 years old. They told us that Everett (their dad), had a younger sister who died of the fever the year before the flood. Her name was Elizabeth and she held the lantern that guided the people to and from the road. It would appear now that Everett and Lizzy are still guiding the town's people; still making the trip between Jonesville and the lake, still searching for a peace they may never find.

Prologue

*A time of simple pleasure, of warm summer days, and cool nights. The smells and sounds of lake front cabin life.
No one can forget that feeling, not even in death.*

Ten: Fishing Buddies

**Since 1946, we have owned property in the Adirondacks and have had a cabin there on the lake for most of that time. This story happened about 10 years after my father's death. He was a carpenter, engineer and could build just about anything. With some help from friends and family, he built our camp and our two neighbors' as well. His hands touched mostly every inch of three to four properties. My father loved it there and every summer he would work non-stop to improve, rebuild, repair and relax at our cabin on the lake. My mother said it was a "Labor of Love." When my father became ill and couldn't keep up the property, he called to tell me he was signing over the property and camp. It was mine now to take care of. He also said he wasn't doing me any real favor though.
I wasn't sure what he meant at the time,**

but I was glad to be honored with the gift from him. He passed away a few months later. It took a lot for me to be there remembering him running around the place fixing, building, and of course playing. But when his day's work was done, he and his fishing buddies, my uncle Ed and their buddy next door, would head down to the lake around 6:30 each night till 12 in the morning just sitting out on the water in a small rickety old wooden row boat. If you remember, the other buddy was Leon my best friend Ron's Dad. One time, I had decided to go up to the lake and spend a few days there. It was fall and I needed to get some things done before closing the camp for the winter. I was working on the camp and had to climb under to look at the piers that the building sets on. I shimmied under and pulled myself to the center of the camp. Much to my surprise, sitting there for who knows how long, was that old rickety wooden rowboat. I tied a rope onto the bow and pulled it out from under the camp. Inside was a surprise as well. I found a set of cushions, fishing poles, a bait box, and two tackle boxes full of fishing gear.

There was a newspaper rolled up and stuck under the seat. Because no real water can get to the center under the camp, the boat and all the contents were virtually untouched from the day my dad pushed it under there. The newspaper date was July 8, 1971. Funny thing that is the date I was to go off to the military, my daughter's birth date and it was the same date my parents threw me a going away party. I still have the invitations that were sent to people for my party. I started looking through the items I pulled out of the boat and opened the tackle boxes. I plopped down in the spot I always saw my dad sitting in while they all sat bobbing up and down fishing. I could see them in the boat from our beach and would wave to them. Without a sound, Dad would raise the stringer of fish to show me their catch. The sun would be down and the glow from over the mountains would backlight the boat and its crew. They always appeared in silhouette to me. I took the gear and put it all away in the camp. I dragged the boat to the beach.

I planned to take it out one more time. I was even going to try to fish. I just couldn't bring myself to do it. It wasn't the same. That night while I was just about falling asleep, I heard a noise outside. Voices, low like they were trying not to wake anyone. They went by the window of my bedroom and faded away as they walked down to the beach. I jumped up and grabbed a flashlight. No one should be using the path and property without my permission. We have had squatters that leave garbage and start fires there. I went to run them off. As I approached the beach, I smelled someone smoking a crappy old cigar. There was something very familiar about that smell. I broke out onto the beach but there was no one there. The stars were bright and the moon had risen to its high point in the night sky. There were a few clouds partially covering the moon so it was like dim twilight on the lake. All I saw was a few small waves as though a duck or a large fish may have just passed by that spot.

**Nothing else.
No one was there.
Not a living soul.**

I went back up to the camp and jumped back in bed. The next morning I went back down to the beach around 7:00am to look around. I liked having a hot cup of coffee and sitting by the water early in the morning. There was never anybody out at that time. You can see your breath as you exhaled and the sun had just risen high enough to cast a few warm sunbeams on the beach and water. The lake was smooth as glass, not so much as a ripple. The carp were out sunning themselves. They looked a little like big, brown logs floating on the top of the still water. I stuck my feet in the lake to let the minnows nibble at my toes. That is when I spotted marks in the sand just under the water. The marks were long straight grooves set in the wet sand. It looked as though someone had launched a boat there. But that was not possible. No one should be using our private beach at all.

I went back up to the camp to start some of the chores I had planned for the weekend, painting, washing, straightening and just plain goofing around. Nothing very important just a weekend alone at the camp. I remembered how many times I saw my dad and my Uncle Ed tinkering with a motor or one of the boats trying to repair the old broken down thing. They would be at it for hours. And without fail, Leon would be right there with them lending his two cents to the equation. Yeah, what a trio. I thought a moment, "Wait a minute Leon? Leon and his crappy old smelly cigars. That was the smell I experienced last night!…. But it couldn't be." I am sure there are plenty of smelly old cigars out there. It couldn't have been him. It was getting dark and time to wash up, get some grub and settle in for the night. Two more days and it's back to civilization and the city again.

The nights are so clear and crisp up here. The peepers (frogs) were extra loud that night. The sounds, the smells and the air just made sleeping here so incredible.

Just like when I was a little guy. I decided to hit the hay a little early and get a jump on the next day. It was about midnight Saturday, and once again I hear the voices just outside my window. Low but very distinctive. Their plodding feet and the rustling of the ground, made it appear like something heavy was being carried. I jumped out of bed and ran out of the camp; tripping over a broom I left by the door that morning. I fell to the ground and made an awful crash. I was sure whomever it was heading towards the beach heard me, and by that time had taken leave of our property. I decided to go down to the lake anyway just to make sure. Again, the night was clear and the moon so bright it cast deep shadows in the woods as I walked. The only sound was a muted splashing from the lake. I broke out onto the beach but didn't see much of anything. Looking up at the night sky was always a favorite thing to do for me. On a night like this, you can see the constellations so clear, it's almost as though you could reach out and touch them. The lightning bugs were out in force that night, and they made it seem like the stars had fallen down to earth and decided to play on the beach right in front of me. I sat down on the sand and laid back to gaze up at the stars. A slight breeze made sure no flying pests bothered me. A few bats circled overhead crunching down on a couple of lone moths that had ventured too far from the protection of the woods. I must have been there for about an hour when I started to doze off. I got to my feet and started to head back up to the camp and my warm bed. I stretched, took one last deep breath of the clear, crisp mountain air and one last look at the lake before heading up. As I turned to go back up to the camp, I caught motion just out about 200 yards off the shore. A black object bobbing around. As I strained my eyes to see what it was, a chill went down my spine and made the hairs on the back of my neck stand straight up. Three people in a small row boat fishing. One of them raised his hand and waved at me. He bent over and held up a large stringer of fish they caught. He placed it back in the water and waved once more, I returned the wave.

I stood there for a few minutes and watched them. They just sat there fishing. I waved once more and they all returned the goodbye.

I turned and started to walk up to the camp. When I had reached the place where the beach met the woods, I turned one last time to look at the fishermen and they were gone.

Vanished!

It only took me a second or two to get from where I was standing on the beach to the edge of the woods. I could see pretty well four or five beaches up and down from ours. They couldn't have rowed that fast. I can't be sure if it was my dad out there or not; but it felt like it was. And for a moment I was back as a kid waving to my Dad as he and his buddies sat fishing to their hearts content. As for the cigar smell, Ron's dad always smoked the most god-awful stinkiest cigars he could find. I went back a few times that weekend to see if I could catch another glimpse of them fishing. It never happened again. I never had the chance to thank my dad for everything he did for me in my life. Teaching me to fish, play golf, and to just live.

I wish I could have told him that I loved him and will miss his spirit. Maybe he knew that and decided to give me one more day with him. One more special moment we could both share.

I took the boat out one last time.
I even caught a fish. I let it go,
jumped in the water and sank the boat.

I am happy for my Dad and his friends.
They will get to fish together, forever or for however long forever may be.

End
(for now)

ABOUT THE AUTHOR

Raymond Feurstein is a retired Communications Engineer.

His hobbies include: professional musician (He plays in a local classic rock band called "Still At Large", teaches music (piano, drums and vocals) woodworking, scuba diving, hang gliding, cave exploring, and gardening. He loves animals and belongs to a few animal rescue groups. He is also a Special Deputy Sheriff for the county. Raymond holds two US patents and three patent pending applications. He is a father of three and has been married to the same incredible woman for 35 years.

Written by:
Raymond A. Feurstein

Copyright © 2012 Raymond A. Feurstein
All rights reserved.
ISBN-13:978-1484058664
ISBN-10:1484058666

Graphic Artist: Terrie Brimingham
Editing By: Christine Wilson
Photographs by: Raymond Feurstein
Book cover photo by: Klaus Sandrini
www.sandrininet.info

Made in the USA
Middletown, DE
13 January 2015